Wl
Working

Law of Attraction

and the Missing Pieces

The Law of Attraction is always at work with our energy. This is an enormous responsibility and can at times be overwhelming. Instead of being overwhelmed with stress, be overwhelmed with joy and excitement. We are all on this ride together and whether you enjoy it or not, is completely up to you.

About the Author

For most of her life, J. Day has helped people while wearing many different hats. Some of these hats are Life Coach, Reiki Master, Facilitator, Public Speaker, Mentor and many more. For her, the greatest joy is in witnessing the blossom of growth of knowledge within another person.

For questions, please email:
Theindigopapillon@gmail.com
Printed in United States

Acknowledgment

This book is for entertainment purposes only. The information in this book is not for diagnosis, treatment, prescription of any physical/mental health disorders. This is also not a substitute for competent and licensed healthcare or financial professionals. Although every precaution has been taken in the preparation of this book, the publisher and author assume no responsibility for errors or omissions. Neither is any liability assumed for damages resulting from the use or misuse of the information contained.

Indigo Papillon Publications
Mailing Address Only
957 Rt. 33 Suite 12
#337
Hamilton Square, NJ 08690

As a special thank you: Visit my website for a **Free Mini Workbook** to get you started on your journey! The link will be on the home page.
www.Theindigopapillon.com
Use code: **Specialthanks**

Why Isn't it Working For Me?

Law of Attraction and the Missing Pieces...

Special thanks to my dearest mother and friend K.L. for your hard work and endless support. To everyone who has been on this beautiful journey with me, I thank you and wish you joy and abundance.

Table of Contents

Preface

- I am writing this as if I am talking directly to you

This book will take a look into the flipside of Light Work and the Law of Attraction. There are missing pieces to the puzzle that leave people frustrated and create a lot of misunderstanding.

Light Work:

Light Work is an umbrella term for anyone who does energy work with a focus on the light. This is a very long list that includes, but is not limited to: Psychics, Mediums, Reiki/Energy Healers, Life Coaches (some types, not all) Teachers, Channelers, Meditators and more. They are often put up on pedestals by the clients who work with them, but are just as flawed as anyone else. This book will delve into their world and the sides that you do not see.

Law of Attraction:

In a nutshell, this is the belief that we manifest everything into our lives through our vibrations. This is a double-edged sword folks. L.O.A. is something that I believe, and have been able to manifest some amazing things. It did not come without a lot of practice and observing others preach, try, and fall very short of lofty goals. The ones who follow these gurus are left feeling both inspired and confused, when it does not work for them.

Part 1

The Back Story

Chapter 1

Light Workers, Gurus and Mentors Oh My!

The Light Worker

These sensitives and empaths are here to raise the vibration of humanity. They are the healers and teachers of the world. Light Workers quite literally use the energy of the "Light/Life" to heal our vibrational selves. I have worked with more than I could even begin to list. Each one has a different story as to how they came to the calling.

It is a calling that is either put up as a paragon of morals and ethics, or one that is seen as the work of a charlatan or con artist. I have been fortunate that almost every person I have met in this field is not out for the money, although most get paid. Nor are they out to con anyone. They truly believe that they are helping people. Oh, there are the con artists that you should watch out for! However, the ones I am addressing here are the ones who genuinely want to help in whatever capacity they are called to assist.

I had a calling from a very young age. I was called to help others in every profession I worked. Helping was part of my family ethics and morals, my parents and grandparents were and are always helping others. They taught me through example, to be of service to the world. My mother always donated her time and energy to the community, and to this day, remains a passionate and devoted contributor to several community service groups. My father was always helping neighbors and friends. If a stranger was in need, he was there to lend a helping hand and his parents were the same.

For me, if family members were in pain I would lay my hands on them and send light. I had no idea what I was doing, but later discovered that it was Reiki. My Reiki Master said that my attunements were a mere technicality, since I had been doing this naturally for so long. I was led to work with the public using coaching, hypnosis, meditation and more. In all these modalities, I was helping others to heal and move on in their lives.

What I am going to talk about in the coming chapters do not apply to all Light Workers, or rather, not all of the issues apply to everyone. It does however speak to a high percentage of them. Perhaps you are one, or you know of one and will find yourself nodding your head in agreement. If you are reading this and do not agree with any of what I am about to say, then you are truly blessed and I am very happy for you. You may however be in a position where you are not aware of the backdrop and that is why I am writing this.

Earth's Little Helpers

Almost everyone I have worked with has felt compelled to help individuals around them. There is one who plays the meditation bowls, because from the moment she heard them, they called to her. She knew this gift had to be shared with others; to give people the same feeling of peace and clarity that she felt from the crystal bowls.

Another Light Worker I know, is a very gifted medium and has been since she was a small child. These messages will come whether you share them or not, so she set on a journey to share them and has not looked back since. She is a great example of someone who, when fame came knocking, turned her back and said no. She has had producers asking her to do reality shows and turns them down each and every time. She wants to keep her work pure and doesn't like what executives and producers do to the process. She does, however, do radio shows and livestreams her sessions, but keeps it to the core of what she does... helping clients heal and connect.

I have friends who do Reiki work, and one in particular, has helped me on more than one occasion. She has this drive to heal like no one I have ever seen. While all of them charge for the services they do, it is always with the deep desire to help and heal others. Light Workers help to rid the world, or at least their small part of it, from pain and sorrow.

It comes at a big cost

Burnout is a word that many of you have heard and possibly even experienced, but this is almost a habit with Light Workers. They shine so brightly that folks gravitate to them like a flame on a dark night. They will take on their energy and will smile through it because it does bring them joy to be of service. Behind the scenes, they are neglecting every one of their needs, including relationships. Yes, this has happened to me! I am writing this from the point of view of someone who had to pull way back and take a break because my health has started to crumble. I am not unique. Go to the social media groups of Light Workers and you will find many who are in the same situation. They often times, do not know it yet, but they will describe the constant fatigue, illnesses, mystery pains, or sudden health crises. There was a very famous Light Worker who wrote about her health failing for the same reason.

Health is not the only cost, if they are not careful, their friendships and social circles, become a thing of the past. Relationships become difficult to maintain and social balance becomes more and more difficult to keep going. This has a variety of reasons. For some they simply may need time to themselves to energetically recover. Others help so many people, due to their inability to say no. Because of this, their own loved ones get put off until later, except later, is a very tricky word. I have worked very hard to avoid this particular trap, and for the most part I have. The energy that was taken away from my life, helping others, was taken from my needs. This will be addressed later in the book.

You will see the same troubles with long-term caretakers, doctors, nurses, therapists, psychologists, massage therapists, and really anyone in the service field. Often times, they are unaware that they are Light Workers. They have found professions that heal the world in different ways. There is a guilt that many will feel if they are taking a moment away from the ones they are caring for. They will eagerly give of themselves and yet have a difficult time being cared for by others. They are often the strongest people you will ever meet, until one day they are not.

The shadows that lingers

You will also notice that in biographies or backstories of famous Light Workers, there are some hard lives. There are many who have come close to death, the tragic early passing of loved ones, addiction, abuse and yet, that is not what you see or feel while around them. If you look closely, you may see the shadows of their pasts in their eyes. You may feel it if you are sensitive as well. Other Light Workers know and will identify it right away. With these difficult childhoods, their sixth senses pop up, (almost out of survival) and carry them to a place where they can fulfill their life purpose.

As they move on with their lives, you may see repeating patterns or extreme highs and lows. This can be a direct result of burn out, or it can come from the relationships they choose. It is often in a later stage that a Light Worker finds themselves in a healthy happy relationship. It is because they are trying to heal the past ones through the new choices. Now this is basic psychology, they will choose friends, romantic partners that mirror past relationships in the hope of healing or fixing them. They may find themselves with those who are passive aggressive, depressed, addicted, verbally or physically abusive, or controlling, out of a subconscious need to make right what they felt went wrong before. There is also a Law of Attraction component to this issue here that we will talk about in the second half of the book.

Each time, as a loved one, you will look on and shake your head asking yourself why? Perhaps you are one of the few they can rely on or you are the Light Worker, who knows all too well of which I am speaking. This is where the missing piece comes in and the part no one likes to talk about, but I will and have, with many of my clients.

Up on the pedestal

Many LW's spend a lot of time up on the pedestals that their clients and loved ones put them on. I have been put up there more times than I can say, and it made me extremely uncomfortable. Because they saw me cry and couldn't handle it, I had to explain that I was human and had all of the same emotions that they did. You may want to put them in a place where they are above reproach. LW's are usually working at a very high vibration, forgive easily, spend their energy healing others and working towards their understanding of the greater good. They are not however, perfect. They will have bad days just like everyone else. They can be jealous, angry, petty, hurt, wounded, and any number of lower vibrational emotions that you can imagine.

It is up to you to take what wisdom resonates with you and accept them for the whole imperfect humans that they are. This is what we must do for everyone we meet. No one is perfect; no one lives their life in a state of grace and perfection all the time. Mother Teresa, who I grew up thinking was humble, pious and had unwavering faith, was far from that. Towards the end of her life, it was discovered that she held serious doubts and her faith was more than shaken, from all that she had seen. This however does not diminish the incredible work she did and the legacy she left behind. She saw and felt things that would shake anyone, and I mean anyone. If we look at her only through the lens of her own disappointment and doubt, then we miss completely the amazing gift of her life's work. We would miss how caring and nurturing she was to those who needed her most. One half of a person does not erase the whole, instead it reminds us that we all have the capacity to be placed on or taken off of a pedestal by someone.

We do this to religious leaders, doctors, athletes, politicians and celebrities. It is not fair or appropriate to do. They are all just ordinary people with ordinary problems. They all have family arguments, vices, health issues, missteps and emotions that make them no better than anyone else. You may have found yourself angry this year that some celebrity said something that you found appalling. Perhaps it was, but haven't you said or posted something that in retrospect, was hurtful or as socially damaging, if you were in their position? Your words can have as big of an impact, if not more so. Your social media accounts are filled with more people you know in person, making your words infinitely more painful to those you are offending. It is easy to judge someone based on position, fame, or celebrity, I challenge you to hold yourself to those same standards, the next time one of your friends tells you that you offended them. Should you lose your job or be publicly shamed?

No, of course not! Yet, we do that to celebrities and anyone of any notability all too often often.

They are in complete truth, no better or worse than anyone else; they are just in the public eye.

Doctors make mistakes all the time, but because people's lives are at stake, we hold them to a higher level of preciseness. Let's face it, there is a lot that modern medicine does not know and may never know. They are limited by the information we give them and the tests and knowledge that are available. Athletes are also idolized and made into role models for kids. The title athlete does not entitle them to a status of role model. They are only physically capable of feats that the general populace is not. That is it folks. They will tell you the same thing if you asked them. Some may have egos that would disagree, but many have come out and said. "I am not a role model."

The pedestal does not allow us to accept the whole beautiful Yin and Yang of a person. Our light and dark selves bring us to whom and where we are in this very moment. When we ignore or admonish those we hold in high esteem, then what are we ignoring and admonishing in ourselves? You are perfectly flawed and flawed to perfection. Your anger, sadness, worries are part of you, yet do not define you. Do not define others by what they allow you to see, or what they will not allow you to see.

The Gurus and Mentors

I use the term Guru like I do Light Worker as an umbrella term for Motivational Speakers, Lifestyle Specialists, Life Coaches and other such titles. Yes I am a Life Coach, not because I am perfect, but because I know how to embrace the imperfections and help those around me to find their inner strength and to heal what is holding them back.

Like LWs, it is important to remember that these gurus are ordinary folk walking a different path. They found something that worked well for them, but may not necessarily work well for you. They want to share with you all of the amazing things they learned and want you to find the same happiness and success they have. Just as it is with a Light Worker, there is a monetary component to much of what they do. This is *called* an energetic exchange; there is nothing wrong with charging for services, even if the end goal is to help others. They share a lot in common with the Light Worker: Countless of them overcame incredible odds, lived through times of darkness, and attract situations/people that are full of negative energy.

Yet, they are the success story you want your path to be. Lifestyle specialists will tell you what that looks like, the Life Coach will help you to discover what is holding you back, and Motivational Speakers will have you jumping up out of your seat with new belief in yourselves.

Before we go any further, I would like to make something very clear: this is not some trash talking expose kind of book. This is to help you put everything in perspective and to remind you that you can be just as amazing. The role of these specialists should be to inspire you and to motivate you, but not to idolize them and to think they are somehow more worthy of the success and happiness than you.

Everyone who has written a book, stood on stage, or run a workshop has had experiences that put them there. They had questions, doubts, struggles and history that pushed them beyond where they were. They each found something special that worked for them, but perhaps what you do not know, is that it worked in one or a few areas of their life, but not others. We are all works in progress; we rise and fall like the tide of the ocean. It is an ongoing juggling act to keep all of the balls in the air; occasionally one or all of the balls fall down. This does not mean that they are frauds or that they somehow lost the magic that got them to where they

were, it means they are human. They, like the rest
of us, need to take a moment to relax, to regroup
and to sometimes start over.

There is a danger to thinking someone has all of the
answers. No one has all of the answers, but if we
take the collective wisdom, put it together, rework it
and turn it over a few times, we might find
something that works for us.

What They Do

A number of these wise folk will utilize the Law of
Attraction. This is the belief that we attract
everything to ourselves, good and bad, through the
power of vibrations. These thought leaders used this
process consciously and unconsciously to get where
they are. They may have read books, listened to
speakers, or had an innate understanding of how
this law worked. From the outside, it may have
looked effortless, and that is how it is once you
have the vibration locked in. What you do not see is
how often they failed, or how many times doubt
shook them to their core. No one will ever really
know but them. What we do know, is that they kept
trying, they kept moving, innovating and adjusting
their energy and attitude, until the right mix was
found.

What you get to see is a carefully crafted final
product that eliminated the muss and fuss. Wouldn't

it be great to see the work that went into it? Wouldn't you love to have an open door to their thoughts as something they tried didn't work? In a way we do, we can look at our own thoughts, feelings, fears and insecurities, and understand that it is exactly the same. The biggest difference is that they pushed through and used everything to make it even better the next time around.

Some simply refused to acknowledge the possibility of failure. They saw each moment, good and bad as a learning experience and as data. They do not take it personally, nor should you. It may feel personal, and others may try to make it personal, but it isn't. Do a vibration check and see are you vibrating with or against this choice. They also follow their gut/instincts and tune into their higher selves. Again this may be consciously or unconsciously, but they do.

The hardest part to remember about the Law of Attraction is that it is always working. It is not about worthy or unworthy, it is about vibrations and energy. You may see those who you feel are unworthy, who are wildly successful, and others who are not, but should be. I know numerous individuals in the second category; amazing, talented people who are completely unaware of their own worth and thus give out a lower vibration, stopping their dreams in their tracks. I also know some who have purposely kept success at bay, because they defined success, not as money flowing in, but as a life well lived. Success and abundance have many definitions, and when you get money out of the way, you can begin to see it is rarely about the money and more about what it represents.

All it takes is watching some videos online and within minutes you will start to see these lifestyle gurus talking about how many cars or homes they have, tempting you into buying their personal map to life success. But those homes, if you look carefully are often empty, staged and barely look lived in. Is that success for you? Where are the family, friends, the pictures, the evidence of the life that they are so excited about. There is evidence of money, and that is it. Abundance is not defined by money and money while wonderful in abundance, does not guarantee happiness.

They may have some answers for you. They may also have nuggets of wisdom, which move you into a better financial situation. This does not guarantee you happiness or stability, and that is where the missing pieces come in: all that is hidden from view, the untold story, and the parts that will help you use all of these other books and strategies to your advantage.

We will go over tools to release old programing that is creating negative self-talk in the second half of this book. The takeaway from this chapter is that no one is perfect and that you are seeing a very small part of the whole. Success in life is based not on worth, but on how you value yourself.

Chapter 2

The Metaphysical Bandage

The biggest mistake many Light Workers and
Motivators make is to use metaphysics and L.O.A
(Law of Attraction) as a bandage for their gaping
wounds. As I said before, many are called to this
line of work after some very hard times. These
times can come in any form: Emotional, physical,
mental, or spiritual. They feel the sense of personal
control that these methods and theories can bring
into their journey. Metaphysics and Law of
Attraction believe in the power of energy and
vibration. We feel that if you can change your
vibration, then you can change your life path. The
problem with this way of thinking is that rarely does
anyone take the time to go over the steps of how
this is done. Often times they may have catchy titles
like: "Change your life in just ten minutes a day!"
or "In just five easy steps you can have more money
than you ever dreamed." The newest ideas revolve
around hacking the Matrix, time jumping or
merging timelines. We are not going into this here,
except to say that they all are missing steps.

The quick fix rarely, if ever, is that quick. I am not
saying that it can't be easy or quick, I am saying
that for most, it is a bit more subtle, more
complicated. They are dealing with way more
internal blocks than they ever realized. This is why
a good Coach never rushes the process. This is why
there are those who go to Psychologists and

Therapists for years. The outside world may see them as foolish, but anyone who has delved into their own dark side knows that it can be a long and winding road until the light begins to shine through. Many will not only work with licensed medical professionals, but also with Light Workers and coaches too. They assemble a team to help them unravel the tangles of the mind and spirit. This is a wonderful strategy! I often recommend that my coaching clients work with therapists, nutritionists, physical trainers and any other professional that will help them on their journey. Having two or three practitioners working together to offer new perspectives and techniques can be very effective, as long as, everyone communicates. The other technique I highly recommend is meditation. Meditation allows everything to float to the surface for you to observe and release.

Back to the bandage on a gaping wound:

Over the years, I have met many passionate and gifted people. As we talked about earlier, many of them held deep wounds. These wounds were the root of their insecurities as practitioners, as well as, their strengths. If they did not take the time to release their issues, pain, anger, grief, sadness, insecurities and negative thought patterns, the tools they learned simply pushed everything below the surface. For a while, they felt empowered, strong, and sometimes even loved/needed. Over time, the facade would crack, and the pain manifested in different ways. For some it was depression, others would lash out in anger. Some even used the very tools that helped them, to hurt those around them. I have witnessed these breakdowns on more than one occasion. More often than not, these are good people, who broke under the weight of their wounds.

It is difficult to watch those you have cared about and looked up to, fall to pieces or lash out against you. I learned to stop putting people up on pedestals and learned that the tools of Light Workers, coaches, and motivators are only as effective as the release work done before it. The theory that changing your thoughts and distracting yourself from the areas that are blocked will allow abundance and joy, to float in, has caused many to be frustrated and angry. They lose faith in the process all together. They have come to me and asked, why isn't it working? I am doing everything right? Maybe it's me, maybe I'm cursed. What am I doing wrong? So many questions! I will answer them all as we go on.

The Law of Attraction is always at work, in your good moments and bad. Vibration is everything, and thoughts are very powerful. If you are inconsistent, if you do not take the problems by the roots, if you hold on to the old, you will only get what you already got: the old - just in a slightly new form. The bandage is a powerful illusion of health. Just like when you were a toddler and you had a little scrape, seeing the bandage made you feel better, even though you never actually needed it. Your body was already doing the job of healing. Your parents knew that the act of putting on the bandage may have soothed your soul, but may not healed your wound.

A deep wound needs a doctor, medicine, time and rest. Placing a bandage over it will not necessarily facilitate healing. Oh yes, your body will try to heal, though if not stitched and cleaned, an infection could brew beneath the very large and deformed scar. The wounds of our soul are no different.

Affirmations, meditation, reiki, hypnotherapy and listening to motivational speakers only help short term if the person is not ready to move on. Do not confuse readiness with desperation. Desperation gets you to the door, readiness moves you through it. In our desperation to get out of whatever situation we are in, we will cling to any idea that promises results. The quicker it is, the better. It is rare that someone slows down and listens to the whole story, reads the subtext and does every step in a way that is authentic for them.

Let us look at Reiki for an example. I am a Reiki
Master and have been a practitioner for a very long
time.

(The following is just an example, not a specific
person/situation)Someone comes to me full of stress
and the symptoms that can come with it. They feel
it in their joints, their digestive system, and may
have headaches. They lay down on the table and I
go to work. I help them to release the worries
weighing them down, sending light to the areas that
are in need. The light travels through their body,
and they feel a wealth of peaceful energy that they
have not felt in a long time. They leave their
session happier and healthier than before and head
right back into the stressful situations or habits that
led them to me in the first place. Do you see the
problem? They were in pain, they were exhausted
from the symptoms and thought that they were
ready to release. Unfortunately all they wanted was
a release of the symptoms, not the problem. In a few
days to a week they will be right back where they
started and end up feeling that Reiki somehow does
not work for them, or that it's a load of bull.

Let's look at the Law of Attraction (L.O.A.) for
another example. This person, in this example, finds
that their bank account keeps hitting bottom, and
that their workplaces never value them. They hear
about this great motivational speaker who teaches

how the power of your thoughts and vibrations can bring abundance into your life. Our hypothetical person takes avid notes, listens to every speaker and question with the most open of minds. They end up feeling pumped, leaving with a fantastic list of tools, easing them onto the path of wealth and happiness. The problem is that they end up listening to the same friends or family members that told them to keep their dreams realistic. To play it safe or that they were in some way not worthy of their dreams. They listen to the same negative energy that started them on the path full of success blocks. One part of their mind knows it's possible and the other part of their mind is afraid, afraid of failure and afraid of criticism. They forget that criticism is a reflection of the one giving it not receiving it. They may not know that criticism can be a tool to hone our skills and better ourselves (not fall into a pity party). Failure is a learning experience, and the true failure is giving up too soon or not knowing it is time to move on. They were desperate for answers and results, but not ready to shift their mind into valuing themselves and changing who they listen to.

The bandage is the idea that these tools will work some sort of magic without having to make any real shifts or changes. You have to be ready to embrace change on every level. Allowing change was the first step to my own healing and balance. Once I embraced change, all sorts of shifts came in to facilitate a huge movement in my life.

Part 2

The Questions and Missing Pieces

Chapter 3

How Much Control do You Actually Have?

Is it Fate, Destiny, Intelligent design, Law of Attraction or just some cosmic free-for-all? This is the question that scholars, philosophers, clergy and layman have been trying to answer since the very beginning. There is no way that one part of one book, even one as fabulous as this, can have the answer to this question. What can happen is that as you read the answers of many, you eventually come to a conclusion of your own. I will give you my interpretation, and you can do with it what you like. Remember that no one person has all the answers, and at the same time all wisdom dwells within.

The ancients personified fate as a form of intelligent design. That the God or Gods have a plan for each and every one of us and that there is no escaping one's destiny. Most of the world's religions have the basic setup that a creator or creators placed us on the earth to live our lives in service to them. Through either a test of faith or service, we show our worthiness to experience a better place either here or later on.

Christianity said that our sins were forgiven because Jesus /God made the sacrifice of his life, so that we would no longer have to offer sacrifices for our salvation. In return, we must offer faith in Jesus/God and walk in the path of righteousness and good will to our fellow man. The ancient Romans and Greeks believed in an afterlife as well, but not as a reward. Rather, appeasing the Gods/Goddesses allowed for blessings here on earth in this lifetime. The Buddhists believe in the cycle of karma and that good works will lead to better and better lives eventually releasing one from the karmic cycle and entering a state of Nirvana.

There are many more religions, but if we look at the ones listed above, we will find that each has a component of God's will and free will. Stating that if we do what is right in the eyes of the creators, we will receive a reward either in this lifetime, the next life, or the afterlife. The problem remains that each religion has different rules for living out this life plan that release our souls back to source. This then means that our salvation could be a mere accident of birth into the "correct" religion. Yet, another problem arises: of all the world religions, which one is "correct?" I see hands raising saying, mine is, mine is!! This could be a fun party game.

Is it possible that all views are describing different aspects of a singular phenomenon? Think good, do good, live in a state of love, find peace with the world around you, and you will get more of the same coming back to you.

The Law of Attraction is not all that different with the exception that we are the creators of our own destiny. Our vibrations attract to us everything on the material plane. This puts the strands of fate in our own hands and not in the hands of another world/dimension deity. In the past, especially in the western belief systems, anything bad that happened to you was seen as a punishment for not living in accordance to God's will. As the world evolved, we understood that illnesses were not a punishment, but a virus or bacteria. We discovered that if tragedy struck, there was usually a traceable cause. We looked to knowledge and science instead of the displeasure of our deities. Our lives depended more and more on what is seen, on the quantifiable, and on the data that was gathered.

So where does that put us today? Well, there are still many theories. Some of my favorites come from the world of science. On the face of it, it seems to make sense. However, if you turn it over and flip it around, it begins to look like a religion. This time, explained by a man of science instead of a man of God.

Here is my take on two of the many theories:

1. **That we are living in a hologram or matrix.**

This could absolutely be the case, but then you must look at the idea of a creator. If this is indeed a giant hologram or virtual reality, then there is a possibility some sort of intelligence created the program…. dare I say God? Perhaps, God is a multidimensional computer scientist. The other side could simply be those that exited the matrix, and there are a few who can hear and see them. Maybe our higher selves are the ones who are sitting at the big simulator and controlling us like an avatar in a computer game. Think about it. There are many computer games where we can create characters and they go off and have jobs, make friends, sleep, eat and work in a second dimensional world. We could be a third dimensional avatar for someone in the fourth dimensions, all shadows of each other living in higher and higher dimensions.

2. Free will is an illusion.

The idea here is that we are completely controlled by biology and external forces, and that free will is simply an illusion. This notion can be seen as far back as the ancient Greeks, and as recently as, Biology professors, like Cashmore. This is another idea that warrants reexamination. We are motivated and moved by our hormones, biological instincts and urges. We have been mentally programed, from an early age, to act and respond certain ways to everyday moments. Milk spills, you grab a towel and clean it up. Why? Because you saw your parents do it many times before. Had you grown up in a different environment, you may have left it for the dog or cat to get, or walked away and let someone else deal with it. That is programing. You do what has been done before. Had you grown up in a home of creative thinkers, you might have added splotches of food dye and made that milk into a piece of art.

This all brings us back to the question of how much control do we have. I think that it is a bit more complex than we are simply carbon-based machines responding to biological and environmental influences. Yes, in part we are, but things like meditation and hypnosis can override those programs. There are many people who push past limits that others, in their situation, would not. You could argue that previous programing, helped the person to turn to practices like meditation in the first place, I would argue that meditation works well for some and not others. There are cases of identical twins growing up, eating the same food, learning from the same parents, having the same genetic/biological programing, and yet they make very different choices. This calls into question the idea of humans being nothing more than biological machines.

For me the idea of a hologram or matrix combines the worlds of science and religion. Perhaps there is a creator, who programmed us to make decisions and live out our lives according to a bigger picture, but that free will is built into that program. Perhaps our choices help us to create our daily reality. This idea also very closely aligns with the Law of Attraction. Your thoughts, feelings and choices bring things to you or repel things from you. I believe that there are fixed moments in our path that will come into our lives over and over again until we address them and make the correct/ designed decision. Everything else is movable and free will based.

Again, I urge you to think for yourselves, and come to your own conclusions. You are intelligent and have a beautiful mind, ready to discover the truth within you.

Chapter 4

Full of Frustration

Our first example comes from a conversation with a client. The tone was of complete frustration. This was a classic example of putting their mentor up on a pedestal, following the directions to the letter and seeing not only their life, but their mentor's getting even worse. They were left feeling angry and as if they had done something wrong. They hadn't, at least not from the information that was given to them: Change your thoughts and feelings into positive ones and your life on the physical plane will become positive, too. That is the nutshell version, but that is it.

I have worked with many clients who were avid believers in the Law of Attraction. They could quote the books and lectures of their gurus and mentors. They did everything right according to the L.O.A. beliefs, but most have left feeling very hindered. Their adoration became disenchantment, and their faith lost into a sea of questions:

- **I have changed my thoughts and dismiss the negative, why isn't it working?**
- **What have I been doing wrong? I say affirmations, and I feel the emotions associated with what I am trying to manifest, why isn't it working?**
- **I have done vision boards, meditations, avoid conflict, do daily gratitude statements, focus on the abundance and still, I am stuck in the same place.**

Do you see a trend here? These are the questions my clients have asked, and often times I have asked myself. None of the activities mentioned are bad or ineffective, but they are missing some steps. When things do not work out the way we want them to, we hear things, like; you must have hidden resistance, negative thoughts, already existing momentum, and other excuses that brush away the bigger problem. The problem is that we cannot see the whole process from the perspective of the person giving the theoretical advice.

Ah, that is the issue isn't it? From up on their podium, their desk, and/or their book, it all sounds so easy. They make it look easy, too. As I said in the beginning, we see the spit and polished version of their lives and what they are presenting to us. There is no possible way to get the entire scope of what a person has gone through, down in a book or into a presentation. During a rather lengthy writing break it dawned on me, that due to the L.O.A., it is difficult for those who that have truly tapped into and figured everything out, to explain how it is they got to where they are. If they did, they may fall out of that vibration and end up right where they were before. To tell the story of your past sorrow, could put you in that vibration, and by doing so attracts more sorrow and loss. This was a huge revelation for me. It also explains why so many people have these brief moments of positive flow and fall right back to where they were. I have been through that cycle more times than I care to talk about. This is why I can talk about it. I can see the bigger picture, and because I am coming out of a low point, I am poised to talk about it without fear of falling. I have never been one to shy away from the heavy emotions. I loved stoking the conversational fires with the forbidden topics. Even on dates, I would discuss the dreaded two: religion and politics. The pastor and Sunday school teachers at church *really* enjoyed my questions. I enjoyed watching people explain their thoughts, and even more, as I got to witness a realization happen. I try to challenge people to look past the obvious and find the hidden truths of their souls.

Even with clients, I rarely give an answer; rather, challenge them to uncover it for themselves. For me, this book is like that. Not only answering my clients' questions, but my own. We can only ever speak from our own experiences and mine has been a beautiful crazy ride full of ups and downs. I understood early on to learn as much as I could from the downs in life. This is where I deviate from many L.O.A. believers; they shy away from the downs. Perhaps this makes things inconsistent for me, but oh the things I have learned, and thus can share with others.

The frustration in and of itself becomes part of the cycle. The more frustration you experience, the more negativity you will attract. The more negative manifestations you experience, the more you lose faith in yourself and feel as if you have done something wrong. You then seek out the help of whoever it is you work with, you get pumped, start bringing in great things to your life and suddenly, bam, life happens. Then the whole cycle begins again.

You are human living with other humans, and like the cigarette smoke from a neighbor's apartment, other people's energy can creep into your house. Oh, you can use air purifiers, charcoal bags, essential oil, but that smell is still there. This is the perfect analogy for what happens to us with L.O.A. We are in our high vibrations, bringing in all sorts of abundance and bam, we run into our boss! He/She is full of fear, insecurity, negativity and taking it out on the ones around them. Perhaps you are cleaning, and you find that old shirt your ex left behind. Maybe birds had a poop party on your newly washed car. What did you do wrong? Nothing, you are fine, but the people and circumstances around you may not be. It is normal for you to experience some effects from this. If you aren't, then perhaps you're disconnecting too much and missing out on the whole being human experience. The ones at the top of the manifesting game often are disconnected or rather connected into something else. There are some who even say that when a loved one or friend is feeling down, they leave them to their own space until they are in a better mood. I understand why, but it can also leave everyone around you feeling as if you do not care, and this can end up manifesting other issues that you do not want.

How you react to and learn from these negative experiences is what is important, not the avoiding. Perhaps it is my Taurean nature, but I run horns first into the negative situations, take it apart and make something new from it. You have that same choice; you can turn away from what is bothering you or stare it in the face, and show it that you are stronger. You are stronger, you may not realize that yet, but I am telling you that you are.

All of life is a series of paths, and each reaction, to any given situation, is a path for you to take. Remind yourself that there is no right or wrong path, only the one you have chosen. You can choose anger, but will it get you where you want to go? Sometimes it will and sometimes it won't. You can choose to let someone think differently than you, that is not your failing, but their choice. You can choose to stay in someone else's negative energy, or move into a more positive one. Each decision will serve you differently and set you on the path that will ultimately bring you abundance of one form or another. We may not always like the abundance we received, but it is there. If you are not enjoying where your choice brought you, then make a different one. Let me give an example:

Choice: Do I stay in a job I hate?

1. If you leave and are angry about it you may manifest another job you hate or worse none at all.
    a. If you choose to leave, but leave with the wisdom that where you are is not a good fit, but appreciate the money, the experience, the people and the lessons, you could attract a much better fitting job.

2. You stay, but remain angry, and possibly bitter. You begin to fill with resentment and end up dreading each day. This could potentially lead to poor reviews and being let go, bringing you to choice #1, but not under your control this time.

3. You stay, make the best of things, throw yourself into work and begin to get noticed

and maybe even reaping the benefits of the attitude change like a job offer somewhere else or upward movement. Again bringing you back to choice #1a, but again putting the control back in your hands.

4. You stay, enjoy the paycheck and fulfill your passion in a hobby or side job.

You see staying and leaving could both lead to great possibilities, it completely depends upon your attitude. This brings us back to what so many gurus say, which is: change your focus, and feel the feelings of a great outcome, and that is what you will manifest. However, there are other things to do that will make it so much easier. This is something that they did naturally and that come easier to some than others. It is that step, that missing piece that I keep referring to. I promise, we will get there and not only will we go over the missing piece, but I will give you activities at the end to help you!

Chapter 5

But I'm so Positive

I am sure you are positive! I am sure that you are practicing everything that you have been told to do. I am sure that you have also had some amount of success with manifesting positive forms of abundance. If you didn't, then you probably would have abandoned ship long ago. You are a trooper who perseveres, and that could be some of the problem. The act of trying is holding onto the old emotions. Let us look at the things you have tried:

- Reiki
- Meditation
- Affirmations
- Vision boards
- Focusing on other parts of your life that are going well
- Going to seminars
- Listening to motivational speakers
- Journaling
- Chakra Cleansing
- House/Space cleansing
- Lists
- Detoxing
- Joining Gyms
- Seeing counselors, coaches or other professionals.

I know I have touched on these activities before, and they can have huge benefits. If you do not look at the underlying problems, then trying these methods can end you up in frustration town and perhaps upset with any of the professionals that you have worked with.

Often, these activities are just a scratch on the surface of a much bigger issue. I can't tell you how many came to me over the years, telling me that some unscrupulous reader told them they were cursed. I had to break the news to them that no, no they weren't. And before you criticize them for believing something like that, it is no different than saying "The devil made me do it." Yes, I do believe that there are dark forces that we don't see, but the darkest and the scariest are the ones that live inside of us. Those parts that are filled with fear, ego, shame, guilt, anger, sadness. Those are the parts that we are told to ignore and look away from. From a very young age, we are discouraged from dealing with those feelings. We are taught to be happy, ignore the hurt, ignore the pain, and ignore the struggle. This is also why we have so many people who are unable to deal with struggle and are shamed into ignoring the darkest parts of themselves.

How often, as a child, were you encouraged to talk about why you had those feelings? Did anyone other than your best friend listen? I was lucky, I had adults around me who would listen, and if they didn't, I made them stop and listen. If you have a child, tell them your feelings on a level that they can understand. Hiding your feelings does not actually help. It can, in the short term, get you through something dangerous or tragic, but afterwards, you must stop and look/deal with those feelings.

As a coach, I help people to uncover those dark hidden areas of their lives, the ones that have been glossed over by happy thoughts and happy faces. Reflect back to when you have done just that, how did it work for you? Were you happier? Did it solve the bigger issues? Did those feelings creep up later, in other situations and relationships? How is the relationship with yourself going? After years of doing this, you can become very disconnected from all areas of your life and even begin to live on automatic pilot.

Waking up every day, stuffing back the words and emotions from the day before, you develop habits to keep that distance going. You may stare endlessly at your phone to avoid conversations and eye contact. You may focus on physical objects and shop too much, keeping yourself satiated with a false sense of control. Maybe food or TV is taking up your time. You can fill in the blanks here. Avoidance comes in all different forms. Hobbies are great until they replace real connections, including the one with yourself.

I speak not only as a coach, who has seen my clients through this, but have been there myself. I speak from very personal experience. I realized several years ago, after a rather difficult breakup, that I had anger issues. I had years of anger stuffed back and built up. I realized this when I broke a punching bag at the gym. A few years later, I had a three day sob fest. After that, I was fine, but I now make sure to keep in touch with those feelings, not hide from them.

Positivity, like everything else on that list, is a tool. However, like the rest of that list, it can be used as a crutch or mask. The world should see the real you and you deserve to know yourself fully. Some of the people I admired most were seen by everyone else as complete jerks. I admired them because they spoke their truth, and often it was the truth, that people around them did not care to hear. Reality can be subjective, but it can also be uncomfortable. While their reality was valid for them, it may not be valid for the person they were ticking off. If it did hit a cord why might that be? Could it be that whoever was offended, didn't like how they looked through someone else's eyes? Had too many around them withheld information to avoid hurt feelings? Positivity can be just as dangerous as negativity. It is all about balance. It is all about seeing the good in the bad and the bad in the good. It is about moving past the social niceties and being real with the people you care about and even some of the people you don't.

I am not telling you to go around ticking folks off. However, being a people isn't doing anyone any favors either.

Think of yourself as a house. If the house has termites, conventional L.O.A. would have you turn your head and focus on the clear parts of the house, or look at other buildings all together. Really, conventional L.O.A. thinking would tell you to change your focus, and the termites will just disappear. The problem is that they have already manifested, perhaps you manifested them or maybe a previous home owner, but the fact is that they are there eating up your house. Ok, put on a smile, get yourself happy and think about something wonderful in your life…. let me know how that goes.

Was that a bit snarky? Yes, yes it was, but hopefully you got my point. Simply being happy will not get rid of what has already manifested. There are steps to get your house healthy again. Once you have done them, then you can focus on being in those beautiful high vibrations. We will bring the termite analogy back a few more times throughout the book, as we look at the different layers and thoughts on the subject.

So here we are now with that final question of the chapter: "Positivity, why didn't it work?" Hopefully, you can answer that question, but if not here we go. Positivity can change things in your life and work as a powerful point of attraction. The things in your past that have already manifested need to be addressed and healed. You can't slap a painting over a hole in the wall and think ok it looks good. Sure, it may look good, but it is not fixed, unless all you care about is the surface. If that is the case, then reading on, may not be for you. Go forth and simply be happy, without actually dealing with the underlying blocks. For everyone ready for some changes, let's keep going!

Chapter 6

When Negatives are a Blessing

Why would I even say that a negative is a blessing? One of the most important components of L.O.A. is the ability to shift your perspective. Often it is conveyed as the idea of simply changing your thoughts. This is problematic for a variety of reasons, one being that we rarely have full control over our thoughts. Sure there are exercises that can train your mind to shift your focus, but as in our termite house analogy, turning your head, does not make the termites go away.

Let's put it a very different way

You are in your house and find that your dog has left a nice stinky gift. Conventional L.O.A. directions would have you walk to another part of the house and sit in a beautiful room, loving life, finding happiness in this and that. Eventually, the odor reaches you in that new room. Every time you walk by that room, you can see it and smell it, but you keep thinking happy thoughts. This is not working at all. You still have that nagging feeling, even if you are out of the house, that you should still be doing something. This is what happens with our feelings and emotions as they move to the background of our conscious thoughts.

We try something else, we say Ok, I don't want to keep walking by and seeing this pile of poop, so I am going to do something with it. You get some gloves and glue and glitter, and you make it the prettiest ball of poop anyone has ever had. Yes it's now a pretty, glittery pile of poo. Congratulations! You covered that thing up, and now you can move on. Unfortunately, the poop is still there; it's covered, it looks better, but the stink shows up on every hot day.

If instead of hiding, changing or avoiding, you could shift your perspective and be proactive. You say to yourself, "Well, looks like my dog's digestive system is working." Then, you clean it up, and get it out of the house. At this point, and then you are free to move on and be truly happy in your home.

Shifting your perspective is not hiding behind positivity or suppressing the negative with happy thoughts. No, shifting perspective takes what is there, turns it over and sheds an even brighter light on the situation.

There is a faulty idea that negative feelings are replaced by the higher vibrational ones. For a very select few, this is the case. However, if it were true for everyone, then every time we found joy after a terrible situation, we would not be pulled back into sadness later on. Instead, the old feelings would be gone and no longer there to assess. If you have ever grieved the loss of a loved one, you know all too well, how your emotions move like the tide. The grief will wash over you, and for a while, you will be overcome and distraught. Eventually, something causes you to smile or laugh, and your heart opens to new people and situations. No matter how good something is, you will be triggered into feeling all of those feelings of loss over and over. Each time the sting is slightly less, you stay in the happy moments longer and longer, but those happy moments and feelings do not replace the loss. The loss begins to fade, as you are able to shift your perspective and see it in a new light. Perhaps you celebrate that their passing means that they are no longer suffering, and that can bring you some peace. Maybe you focus on them being in a better place, or that you can still feel their energy with you. Everyone has something different. Instead of your perspective being that of a victim who has lost a loved one, it is that of someone who has loved deeply and can see the joy in having had them in your life at all. This comes with time, patience, and the choice of looking at it differently.

The recent past has been a story of negative blessings for me. I had been having a cluster of health problems that I finally sat down and went over with my general practitioner. He was smart enough to venture a guess at a pituitary adenoma (tumor). After many tests and arguments with my insurance provider, sure enough He was right. All of those awful symptoms were blessings that pointed to a potentially serious issue. Another doctor put me on medication that seems to have shrunk it, and those symptoms are now all disappearing. I will know if it is gone in the fall. Now this diagnosis had me a little freaked out, even with such a great prognosis. But the medicine and the health issue forced me to make a decision that I had been putting off for well over a year. I closed down my Center. I had this Center for over seven years, and I made the move to go completely online. The medicine had potential side effects, that would have made keeping up such a hectic schedule quite difficult.

A few months after the decision was made, I was diagnosed with stage zero breast cancer. You see, closing down the center became a new blessing. The timing worked out in such a way that I was not stuck in a yearlong lease. I was able to take the time for radiation treatments without freaking anyone out or losing clients.

The irritating part of L.O.A. comes in with the ones who tell you to just think the cancer away. I had quite a few telling me to heal myself. Some told me not to even acknowledge it, and it will disappear. If my car has a popped tire, I cannot think my way into the tire re-inflating and the puncture going

P a g e | **63**

away. The popped tire has already been manifested into the person's reality, they cannot un-manifest it. They could manifest a tow truck or a passerby with a spare tire, or the money to buy a new one. That is the cancer already manifested, yes, I could manifest healthy tissue and a healthy body, but now that the cancer is in my consciousness, the more I "try" to heal it, the more I am cementing it into my consciousness. I could try and think about something else, but the diagnosis already entered my reality. I have to take care of removing it and beginning again to see my body in a perfect state of health.

The other problem with people who were saying this, is that they were missing the blessing hidden in all of this. The bigger picture is that I was extremely overworked and stressed. My health was a warning sign of a potentially scarier problem, stress. Had I not had the tumor or the cancer, I would still be driving over 300 miles a week for work functions, speaking engagements, and meetings with clients. This forced me to slow down and listen to my body in a way that I had not before. Now, if I need to nap, I nap. When I need to sit down and have a cuddle sesh with my dog, I do. The cancer was curable, the potential high blood pressure, and possible heart attack that would have been in my future are harder to detect and overcome.

If you tell someone who is sick to think themselves well, you are in a very well-meaning way, shaming them. At the same time, you are missing a much bigger picture of which you are entirely unaware. My ability to shift my perspective kept me healthier and happier through the radiation, than trying to cure myself with avoidance and forced joy. I am still feeling the lowered immunity with colds and infections, but I acknowledge them as a side effect of a step I took to protect and heal myself.

I was sharing this part of my book with a friend today, and she had something to add. Her mother was diagnosed with a very difficult to cure cancer, 6 years ago. They were very proactive, using both western and eastern methods. She had a procedure, and it along with a change in nutrition, helped her to heal. My friend brought up the fact that a very famous person also had the same type of cancer, put off the treatment that her mother had, and used only alternative therapies. Her mother is now a six-year survivor and the other person unfortunately is no longer with us. I am not saying this to negate alternative therapy, but rather to say that perhaps we can be proactive with all forms of treatments and change our thoughts as well. She used both and survived.

As a Reiki Master, (yes, an alternative therapy and no, not a cure) it is not my job to heal, but to send light where it will do its best work. I tell my reiki students that they should never try to heal an illness, for it could be a warning sign for a patient's doctor to discover and heal a bigger issue. The reiki practitioner who thinks they healed a cold, in fact just possibly removed the one symptom that could have told the doctor that this person has Leukemia or Thyroid cancer. In fact the niece of another friend of mine was diagnosed with Leukemia in just that way.

This can be demonstrated again with the termite analogy. You find those termites, and as you tear down walls, and you find faulty, dangerous wiring. Did the termites just destroy your house, or help you save it? Perspective, blessings are all in the perspective.

Changing your focus	Shifting your perspective
• Looks in another direction	• Looks at the same direction in a new light.
• Avoids	• Acknowledges
• Overlays positive onto the negative	• Gives voice to the pain, but brings out the benefits

Chapter 7

When Helping Others Hurts You

Yes, you read that chapter title correctly. There are times that helping others can be harmful to you. This does not mean that I am telling you to be selfish and self-absorbed. As I stated earlier in this book, I was raised in a family where helping others is as natural as breathing. However, there comes a point in which this urge can be keeping you from your own health and happiness. L.O.A. states that what you think and feel comes to fruition, so what are you sending to the Universe, if you choose to not give back to yourself? I will lay it out over the course of this chapter.

We have an innate urge to help our fellow man and generally frown upon those who do not have or follow that urge. We see them as selfish and self-absorbed, but is that really fair to think, if we do not know their whole story. Perhaps you are meeting the person who came out of a toxic environment and for the first time is attending to their own needs. From the perspective of a newcomer, they may seem cold and uncaring, but in reality, they are finally caring for themselves. This urge is natural as we are social mammals and if we see a weaker member of the group, we wish to help them along to make the whole group stronger. This is a very primal urge. We see this behavior in other animal groups, so it is not surprising to see it in our own. One internet search can help you to find videos of a herd of elephants helping their young out of a hole, or a dog sitting by their friend who has been injured. Baby animals have large wide set eyes, to help us kick in the nurturing instinct. It is programmed into our biology.

You can also find this programming on a social level. Many cultures revere the elderly; the younger generations take care of the older generations. It is my belief that the western world should adopt more of this attitude. We have crowdfunding, social media fundraisers, governmental aid and religious charities. Those are just a few of the social systems in place, where we make it clear that "we care." We do, and we should.

There are numerous benefits to caring for your fellow man. It is empowering to help someone in need. We often see it as paying it forward and feel as if we are passing along the favor. I did that many years ago. I was in a bad car accident almost 15 years ago on the coldest day of the year. The car spun out on a patch of ice and hit a tree. My window smashed in and cold air was filling the car. This elderly gentleman, who was on his way to meet his son for breakfast stopped and stayed with me until help arrived. He offered me his gloves. I thanked him and told him that I was ok, but the fact that he stayed with me was very touching. I never got his name, but many years later made a donation to a place that I used to work at, for flowers to be planted in his honor. His help inspired me to spread some of that beauty along the way. Now he will never know, but some part of me hopes that he will someday pass by those flowers and smile. His kindness was so natural, but meant so much. In that moment, his actions connected two strangers and made the world a better place.

I have known many to take care of their parents and grandparents as they age, and never once have they said it was a burden. The sentiment was always one of being an honor. However, you could see the wear and tear, the chronic fatigue, and energetic toll it took on them. They do feel that empowerment, the love, the bonding and sense of accomplishment of being in that position. Both parties benefit greatly when help is offered with and open and joyful heart.

The flipside is often not discussed. Giving your time to others often keeps you from self-care. When at the beck and call of family and friends, ask yourself, would they return the favor? Sometimes this is impossibility, because of health or finances. There are those that you drop everything to help them move, deal with a drama, offer advice or free services and when you are then in need of help, they are nowhere to be found. You need to start questioning why? Are you trying to keep the relationship, through your help? Are they relying on

P a g e | **70**

you instead of their own resources? Have they asked anyone else, and you are the only one who says yes? You may want to reevaluate this relationship. Often times, these one-sided relationships fizzle out when you are unable to do all of the work you were doing, and guilt ensues if you have something to do for yourself. You end up sacrificing time with those who are supportive, or you miss out on your own opportunities. You also, at the same time, enable them to remain in the victim state, when they could stand on their own two feet.

Saying, "Not now, how about tomorrow/next week/next month," can be your greatest tool for this kind of relationship. It gives them time to figure things out for themselves and allows you to have a personal life. It also lets them know that they are important to you and that you will give them time at a later date, when it is convenient for you. A parent who does everything for their child may be depriving that child of learning life skills that would make them a stronger, self-reliant adult. If you wouldn't want that for your child, then why take that empowerment away from your friends and family. If you are that parent, stop it and give your child some credit! They are strong and capable if you let them. You would be very surprised at how much they can do and at a very young age if you give them the tools. It also teaches the people around you that it is ok for them to take time for themselves. Bringing this back around to L.O.A. Saying "Not now, how about later?" Is sending a strong clear message that you are making yourself a priority. You will then begin to attract people and situations that make you a priority as well. You may lose some along the way, but chances are they were using you. Now that you are no longer useful, they have moved on to someone else, or even better, they started to do things for themselves.

It does not matter the situation, self-care is vital! If you do not take care of yourself, then that is when the situation becomes toxic. The person/people you are caring for can become the excuse for everything that you are putting off. You must ask yourself: Are you truly helping, or are you using this situation to avoid your needs and your life. Are you allowing the help that you are giving to become the reason, you don't take that job, class, enter into a relationship, etc.?

Long-term care situations are different, and we will cover that later. I am speaking of the toxic relationships where you are so busy listening to, caring for, or helping out other people/person that you quite literally do not take opportunities that will benefit you. This is because you are afraid that choosing anything over the person could ruin that relationship or because you are so busy with their lives that you don't even see the gifts the universe may be offering you. This is sending the vibration out that you are not the star in your own movie. Shouldn't you be the star in your own movie and not the supporting actor? In addition, using somebody's reliance on you as an excuse, is unfair to them. You are making that choice to be at their beck and call. This choice, that you are making, can eventually cause you to resent them. If you shift the balance a little, you will see big changes. If they can't respect the change, it's best to move on and let them figure it out.

The other part that can become toxic occurs when you become their reason that their life is not working out. When you start helping someone, you do not think of it turning around on you. You cannot fathom how they could become angry with you. This has happened to me. Several years ago, I had someone who I thought was a friend stay with me. They told me they were in an abusive situation at home and asked if they could stay with me. The understanding was that it would only be a few weeks while they got on their feet. Needless to say, six months later they were still with me. There were several job opportunities in town that would have afforded them time to look for even higher paying ones. Their exact response was that doing those jobs would be "Soul Sucking." My thought was; isn't staying on my couch soul sucking? Clearly, the answer was no. They proceeded to bad-mouth me to all of my neighbors. Eventually, when I started asking for rent six months in, they conned their way into another place. I found out many years later that they did the same thing to the next unsuspecting soul. I had opened my home to this person, and they said I was a bad host for not feeding them and paying off their bills. That was not, nor would ever have been the arrangement, since they were a capable adult, and I had enough issues paying my own bills. I share this story, to let you know how easy it is for well-meaning help to get turned around on you.

I have been focusing on relationships, but all of this goes for charitable work and donating your time as well. It is a great thing, until it takes over your life. I know quite a few, who spend so much time on their charity work and organizations, that they have not only the problems mentioned above, but they also use it as a way of escaping their own problems. They seek refuge in the problems of others. It keeps them at the surface of their own life and prevents them from progressing. They will deal with it later. I am sure you know someone like that. They never deal with their feelings; they are too busy helping others with theirs. They put off big changes because they are "Needed," somewhere. They miss time with family, friends and themselves, because they are off helping yet another person or group. By the time they talk to someone like me, they are so entangled that they can't see a way out. What was once a place of solace and reprieve became a form of escapism.

Now, what about those who find themselves in a situation where they are providing long term care for a family member or friend? This is both an important role and one that can have all of the effects we spoke of earlier. It does not have to though. Maybe you volunteered to take on the caretaker hat or maybe it was thrust upon you, but no matter how it happened you must create a plan to make sure that you:

1. Do not get burnt out
2. Do not put your life on complete hold
3. Become the focus of anger or resentment from the one you are caring for or other family members
4. Do not make them your excuse for not doing what you need to do for you.

One of the fears is that something will happen when you are not there. This is a valid fear, but one that could be an issue if you are even in another room, if you have a job, or if you are out running errands, something could happen. You are not in control of that. Let's flip the script; something could happen to you too. Let that fear go, and just be prepared. Do what is in your control and trust that you have done everything possible to make sure that they are cared for while you step away.

It's old fashioned, but make a list or a care chart, it works for hospitals. Post it in a easy to see area, so that if someone else steps in, they know what needs to be done and at which time. Also this will help you organize the chaos of what can be a complex situation. Schedules for: medicine, appointments, meals, hygiene, leisure activities and self-care should be on this chart. You should write in time for you, so that your needs can be met. Are you keeping up with your doctor's appointments? Are you eating, sleeping, and making space for your own goals?

Recognize that you need a team. Maybe you can rotate with another member of the family? They should spend time together as well. If you are the only one available you must have a plan for care when you are taking care of your needs. If they do not have the means for a full time nurse, maybe hire one once a week or once a month, to give yourself a day just for you.

Instead of focusing on what you can't do, focus on what you can. Being a caretaker can offer you the kind of time with a person, which we often don't get as adults. As adults our jobs and lives take us away from quality time with our loved ones, this can be a moment to take it back. You can also pursue hobbies or other interests in your downtime. Any hobby that can be done in one location can be done in your downtime. Writing, reading, yoga, cooking, gardening, sewing, knitting, online learning, the list is endless. The point is, if you must stay in one location for extended periods of time, you will have downtime, while they are sleeping, physical therapy, visiting family and friends. Build it into the schedule and you will find that you can create new opportunities for yourself, perhaps ones that you were not even expecting.

You have so much potential and being of service to others is just one facet of that. Giving back can be a part of who you are, but no one wants to see you stop your own progress. Remember, the further you go, emotionally, mentally, spiritually, physically, and socially, the more you have to give. An empty battery can't fuel anything.

Chapter 8
The Missing Piece

Here we are at the missing piece, that is Release! We touched on it and many times our L.O.A. Mavens, Coaches, Gurus will hint at it, but never come out and say it. As I have said before, to release or even talk about release can be a bit counter-intuitive to the Law of Attraction philosophy. It means sitting in the old/negative energy, which, to many people is a no no. You are supposed to just forget that whatever is blocking you exists. Like our home with termites, this does not work. You must remove the rotten wood and get an exterminator in that place, then rebuild. If you slap new wood and paint onto the old structure, sure you have a pretty picture, but in the end, the house is still falling apart.

What does release even mean? The "what" is simple, it is letting go on an emotional, physical, mental, and spiritual level the following: Cords, programs, people, situations, emotions and anything else, holding you in old toxic patterns. The "how to release" is a bit of a tougher question. There will be a free downloadable mini-e-book on my website to help you with that, as well as, a full companion workbook that will be available in Fall/Winter of 2019. The reason that I am not listing it all here is that there is no one answer, no quick fix. Every person and every situation is different. What works for you on one issue, may not work on another. This is a process, and it is an important one. If you are still uncertain as to the importance of releasing, read my example below. If not, read anyway, it may help you to help someone else!

Another analogy I have used with my clients is the following: You have a dinner plate; you notice that there is some mold and rotting food on it. You do not acknowledge it, because that would be "Giving it power," so you put delicious healthy food right on top. You bring this beautiful plate full of yummy fresh food to your table and you sit down to eat from it. Sure, the food on the surface may be okay to eat, but all the food on the bottom of the plate has been contaminated and will make you sick. Are you going to eat from that plate? The problem is that while your thoughts may have changed, your body has not. Our bodies have muscle memory, this is why practicing at a sport generally can help someone get better, but when a kid has a growth spurt they often have trouble playing, because their muscles remember the moves, made back when they were shorter. Your emotions can stay with you physically, so can negative people, situations, and circumstances. Your body will recall the pain, or hold onto it. You may notice emotional releases during massage or yoga. You are quite literally releasing old emotional issues in a physical way.

Release can take as long as you need. This is a kin
to grieving. No one can tell you how long to take.
They may try and with good intentions. They may
urge to move on from a situation, because they want
to see you happy again. They may be frustrated with
the persistence of your emotional or energetic state,
but this is not for them to worry about. I will state
again that there is a difference between dissipating
and dwelling. Sometimes we need to talk it out, we
need to give voice to our feelings, but if that voice
begins to overpower your everyday life and infect
other relationships, then you need to ask why you
are holding on. How are you gaining from holding
onto that emotion or situation? Is it somehow
protecting you from better versions of that situation
such as new jobs or relationships? Does it make you
feel more interesting in conversations, as if it
somehow defines you? Why let what is blocking
you take up any more real estate than it already has?
Your thoughts and emotions have been tied up in
whatever this is, are you going to give it more of
your energy to potentially destroy? No, give it a
voice and see it leaving you when you do! You have
said it, now it is gone. Dwelling in pain gives it a
breeding ground to grow and take a more permanent
foothold. Ignoring it completely can do the same
thing, except it crawls beneath the surface where it
can be difficult to detect. It takes a balance. In the
workbook I will go over many activities and steps

to this process: Process/Acknowledge, Release, and Allow.

One of the most difficult things to let go of is Old Programming. Programming is those thoughts that have often been with us since childhood. They can come in at any point in our lives. Here are some examples of programming:

- Money is difficult to earn.
- When I reach this goal, I will be happy.
- When I fail at something, it means that I am a failure.
- Starting over is a failure.
- Happiness is unreachable or for other people.
- I must do what others have done before me to be secure and happy.
- My____ was a victim, so I must be one too.
- Money, stability, and love equal happiness.
- Struggle is bad.
- It's up to fate.
- The future is fixed.
- You can't have it all.

These are just a few examples of faulty or bad programming. The most successful people in the world have found a way to release this programming. When I say successful, I mean in all areas. Now those who are successful in one area, but not another, may have to release other programs. Perfect is a dangerous word, because it eliminates the need for evolution and growth. When the people you view as successful have reached one goal, they are usually onto another. My favorite example of this is Oprah. She is constantly evolving and challenging herself. She easily could have sat on her laurels, as a talk show host, and let that define her to the public. Instead, she has worked on every aspect of herself. She has worked with some of the most prominent spiritual leaders of our time; she has worked on her physical health and emotional health. Yes, clearly I think she is an incredible example, but also know that as we spoke about earlier in the book, a person who underneath it all, still has issues to deal with. She has, however, released and continues to release the old faulty programming that so countless people wanted to place upon her. She had many odds against her, but rose above in every possible way. And yet, here she is still evolving and challenging herself.

Many other public figures have released/rejected faulty programming to get where they are. Here are some others: J.K. Rowling, Abraham Lincoln, and Michael Jordan. All of them were rejected, failed and told by someone that they weren't good enough. That is a program that others tried to place on them and not only did they reject it, but went on to prove every one of the haters wrong.

Their stories are unique, but their throwing off of old paradigms, programs, and other's bad energy is not. There are so many individuals throughout history and perhaps right next door that are living out extraordinary lives, and you may never even know it. You may hear words like challenge, bravery, adversity, but the people living these amazing lives do not. Instead of a challenge, they see lessons. Instead of adversity, they see fuel to push them further. They live their lives with confidence and in their own truth. I loved working retail, because I would get to hear some of these stories and meet some of these amazing folk; they're everywhere. Any single parent busting their butts to raise happy healthy kids is releasing and has released some part of who they or others thought they were.

Every person who finds joy in their day to day lives and lives in a state of inner peace has released what was holding them back. Anyone who has fought their way through a health problem, either chronic or acute, is releasing every day. I am almost all healed and had someone tell me how brave and strong I am. I don't see it that way. I see myself as blessed, and I choose to learn from everything that has happened. I released the fear and sadness that came over me; even had a few panic attacks. Once I stepped back, saw the bigger picture, had a good cry, I moved on and became proactive. I acknowledged that I was sad, scared and angry. Tears and anger are not forbidden negatives to be avoided, they can be very healing. They are an important part of releasing anger and grief. Once you fully acknowledge these emotions, you are ready to forge a path with those new positive thoughts that will bring you the positive abundance that you are seeking.

I also dealt with the passing of someone very close to me, who fought valiantly and lost her battle with the same illness. She was positive and graceful, but I knew from speaking with her that she made peace with all possible outcomes. I am still releasing the emotions that come with grieving and taking lessons from her beautiful journey. The point is:

1. Release is important
2. Releasing is a process
3. There is no set timeline
4. Successful people have done this work not once but over and over.
5. People are successfully releasing old programs and patterns all the time.
6. Success is not defined by money, rather the ability to shake off other's expectations and

limitations and to walk away from all that could potentially hold them back.

I do not think that I can stress enough, that amazing successful people are everywhere. You just need to tune in, listen and learn from them. Then go and forge your own version of success.

Chapter 9

Old and Faulty Programs

Let's talk about each of the programs I listed and why or how they are faulty. As we go through each of them you may identify with these beliefs and that is the perfect time to let it go, with the understanding that those beliefs are no longer serving your highest good.

"**Money is difficult to earn.**" Is it? You find it on the street, you can find and sell scrap metal, just lying on the street for pickup, you can earn money while shopping. I have a friend who is a super couponer and gets grocery carts full of items for just pennies, sometimes even getting money back! Financial abundance is everywhere; we live in a day and age of the internet. People are literally selling things they do not have in their possession and making money. Yes, you need to know how to do these things; the information is out there. The Universe has unlimited resources, and we are the ones who put restrictions on things. Even in the deepest part of the recession, I saw people on unemployment saying that there were no jobs, and yet, when I would point to hiring signs, they would say it is not enough money. I even dated a few gentlemen who said those exact words, yes more than one. You have no money, they are hiring, and you say it's not enough? What is enough? Ask yourself why you are putting up a block against money if that is where your struggle is. Is it because you saw your friends and family struggling, and you want to be just like them? Is it because it is just what everyone else says? Just this month, I got two, not one, but two check in the mail because my insurance made a mistake and they rectified it. Now, I could have been focused on their mistake and how they had been taking too much, but instead I rejoiced at the financial abundance flowing in. Do you see how money literally came unexpectedly out of the blue and two times from the same company? This has happened a few times. Sometimes a new client that comes out of nowhere. Opportunities for money are there, you just have to be ready. Instead of saying, "It's not enough," say, "It's a start!"

"When I reach this goal, I will be happy." No, no, no, no, no this is the worst statement I have ever heard. Why on earth are you putting off your happiness? It is everywhere and it is a choice. Sometimes you have to push yourself to make it a priority, but it is worth it. I have been overweight my entire life and for years I said, I will be happy when I am thin. You know what? I know plenty of thin people who are not happy. Problem solved, be happy now. You are either a happy person or you are not. Nothing external can bring you happiness, because it is all temporary. Everything is fleeting, so if you place your joy and peace upon something that is temporary, then your joy will be temporary, as well. See the problem? The other issue is that we are constantly setting new goals and lines in the sand for which, then we shall be happy. I am sorry, but you will keep moving that line until finally one day at the end of your time, you will look back and wish you had been happy when.

"When I fail at something, it means that I am a failure." Nope when you fail at something you are a student of life, an experimenter, a scientist. You are learning what works and what doesn't. We tell children that if at first you don't succeed….. That goes for you as an adult too. Stop with the pity party, turn it around and see what went wrong. Try it again and see if that works. Now I do not suggest this method for trying to outrun an angry cheetah. You will not win. I do however recommend this with relationships, careers, style choices and many other areas. I will admit after several attempts at making cookies, I am rubbish, but I did find one cookie recipe that I am fantastic at! So I stick with that and try other things in the kitchen. Years ago, I made a wreath, the outcome was terrible. This year I tried again, I looked at a few tutorials and success! Most of my crafting adventures have gone like this. Have fun, enjoy the failures as potential internet memes of DIY gone wrong. Life is messy, but failure is simply a new start in disguise.

"**Starting over is a failure**." It is very easy to feel like a failure when you have to give up a dream or begin again. It is just a chance to learn something about yourself or the situation. If it is a relationship, then it has just run its course and is no longer serving the highest good. When you hold on to a situation, person, or idea that is no longer right for you, then you are keeping yourself from other opportunities. When you stay in a job that you hate or are mistreated, then you are telling the universe that you do not deserve to be in a place or position that makes you happy. You are sending the message that you believe that this is how you want to stay. The more you complain and anguish over your mistreatment instead of just starting over, then the further away you push new and potentially better opportunities.

Starting over is a chance at some new adventure. It's a clean slate that for a while, may be difficult to adjust to, but it could lead to exciting new opportunities. I found myself in that situation many years ago. It was bad from day one, but I was determined to make it work. Other people told me to get out while I could, but I was stubborn. As a result, starting over was thrust upon me. There I was interviewing and sending out applications. It took me two more years to end up in the position that I have now, and I have never been happier.

Everything fell into place, and I realized that I had to learn that lesson of "staying too long," so that I would not do it again. This goes for relationships, friendships, housing, you name it. Everything in its time, and if you can make peace with change, then starting over can be a blessing!

"Happiness is unreachable or for others." Is that so? Is happiness for other people? It is for and can be for anyone who decides that happiness is a priority. As I said before, it cannot be based on anything external or conditional. If you place happiness up on one of those awful pedestals that I told you not to use, then yes it will forever be unreachable. This does not mean that you will walk around forever happy with a smile plastered on your face, but it does mean that when life gives you a challenge, you can choose to see some silver lining and focus on that. You can be angry or sad for a while and then release it to find the opportunity or benefit to what is happening. You may have had a difficult start, and it is easy to become angry, negative or feel abandoned by the world when you have been dealt one bad turn after another. Just remember, you do not have to let it affect the rest of your life. I have personally known and worked with a number of "Cycle breakers." They chose to live on their own terms and not allow, the hand that was given to them determine their life path. They fought and grabbed for their joy and light. Yet, there are those who with every opportunity afforded to them, complain and just want more. They will never be satisfied unless they decide to allow happiness in. It is like keeping your blinds closed and curtains drawn and then complaining that there is no light.

"I must do what others have done before me to be secure and happy." This is another one that people get stuck in. I am childless, not by choice, but by circumstance. I was sitting in a car with my friend and a friend of hers. They were talking about how getting married and having children is just what you do. That was what her parents did and her grandparents before them. She, my friend's friend was saying that that is what people did to be fulfilled. Others have said it's selfish to decide to be childless. I could have argued that it is selfish to have a child, because that's what all of your friends are doing and not because you actually want them. She was so blinded by tradition that she made her choices according to someone else's plan and is still not happy. My close friend, who was there, has said that from watching me and another one of her childless friends she can understand how your life can be fulfilling even without a family and children. I am happy to be a great example, but as I said happiness is a choice. I always thought that I would be married and have children by this age, but life took a very different path, and I have found a way to be happy in that path. Not settle, oh no. There were chances, but the men I had dated at that point, were not ones that I could see myself spending the rest of my life with, so I didn't. Instead, I found joy in my career, mother the heck out of my dog, and know that the right relationship will present itself when I am ready.

Other examples are illustrated when people follow the same schooling and career paths as their parents; it feels safe because, once again, it is familiar and it is tradition. If it made them happy, that is wonderful, but those choices were theirs to make, now you have yours. We live in an age where the world is at your fingertips. You can learn online, you can start businesses online, you can build empires with very little startup, because the online world has brought opportunities to the average person that would not have been available even 25 years ago. You can absolutely play it safe if that is what makes you happy, but do not think that what you know will be the same 5, 10, or 15 years from now. Once safe stable careers are now fading into the past as technology rises. The family unit is changing and evolving, as our ideas about relationships and even gender are changing. Clinging to the perceived "safe" situations and choices can make you vulnerable when change eventually comes marching through. Make your own choices, and understand that what worked for your family or someone else, may not be your best choice.

"My___ was a victim, so I must be one too." We touched on this in the previous two sections. We grow up, often seeing people we love, hurt and abused. This imprints on us in a way that it is difficult to extract from our subconscious. I have seen entire families, generation after generation finding themselves in abusive situations. Sometimes they are staying for the perceived security. They are afraid that they will have no money, or that they will disappoint their families with a failed relationship. Often religious views are misconstrued to make people believe that they would be disappointing God.

As someone who was raised in the church and has actually read the Bible: When entering a marriage they tell you to obey the husband as you would Christ. They often fail to state that the Husband is supposed to emulate Christ. If you are a believer in the Bible, then you would know that Jesus was not abusive, neglectful, or hurtful.

That is just an example of one religious view. There are many, but most religions around the world hold that you are to love and care for one another.

Anything else is just someone twisting holy words to try and validate their own abusive behaviors.

Be the cycle breakers, leave behind the hurt, anger and abuse. Forgive and let go. Start by loving yourself. Start by treating yourself the way we all deserve to be treated: with, love, patience, understanding, forgiveness, time and generosity. If you can light that self-love light up, people will gravitate to you in a beautiful way.

You can forgive those who hurt you, but that doesn't mean you need to stay. If you have children, ask yourself, what kind of life you want for them and start setting the positive examples. You have to walk the talk, not just hope that they will figure it out somewhere else.

"Money, stability, and love equal happiness." Stability is like the tree that can bend in the storm. The ones that are hard and unyielding to the weather around them usually end up snapped in half, creating a lot of damage as it goes. Money is energy, it is an idea. Money is no longer backed by gold and therefore no longer a physical thing of value. It represents the idea of energy, service, or product having an arbitrary value set by the community as a whole. Stability is an illusion that we can control all circumstances in all areas of our lives, when clearly this cannot be done.

Two years ago, I had just paid off my car and I was thinking woohoo, awesome, no car payment and bam, car was totaled in one second by a tree in a storm. I know I shared this story earlier, but here is a different look at the same incident. Now we will look at how life can change in a second. I dutifully paid off my car and was about to work up a savings and the Universe had gone and rewrote the script. The best actors, teachers, doctors, nurses, cooks etc. are not the ones who have everything memorized, but the ones who can improvise.

The only instance where love equals happiness is the one where you love yourself unconditionally. I have brought up my dog, and yes, that little guy has filled my heart and healed it in ways I didn't even know were possible. However, we all know that our animal friends do not live for our whole lives. They are a reminder that love is precious and to be treasured. We hold it, as if holding water in a cupped hand. You open up to it, but holding on tight causes it to slip away. We become so worried that we forget to be in the moment and enjoy. When I hold my dog, he is not thinking of belly rubs that he may get tomorrow, rather the belly rub that he is getting right now. They live in that state of right now. We could all do that a little more.

"**Struggle is bad**." Struggle is what has led to the world's inventions, evolutions and progress.

Struggle is not some bad evil to be avoided. L.O.A. gurus will sometimes state that there is no need to struggle, that with one thought we can manifest the entire world. Yet, we are also told that contrast can show us what we truly want. So which is it? Contrast is a pretty word for struggle, for that which we are trying to change. That contrast or struggle is what causes us to change our thoughts in the first place. Struggle pushes us to improve, to look for better and easier ways to navigate our lives. Yes, the struggle is real and yes, it is good.

"**It's up to fate.**" We spoke of this in the chapter 3. Our fate is changed by the choices we make, thoughts we think and the feelings we act upon. Our fates intertwine with those around us, choices upon choices tumbling onto one another, each life creating another ripple in the pond touching the other ripples around it. Sometimes they are in sync and other times bumping into one another. If you stay still, then those ripples will never form and fate has nothing to work with. You must take a step and make a move in order for fate to reveal all the paths that you can choose. How quickly you progress and what path you take is ultimately up to you. A writer, who never writes, is just a thinker. A singer, who never sings, is just a member of the audience. If you have a hunger for something new in your life, then for God's sake, feed it. Do not wait for the celestial delivery truck to magically show up with food. Law of Attraction cannot function properly to bring you what you asked if you do not follow the pulls and urges of your soul.

"**The future is fixed**." We have already talked about this extensively. The future is not fixed. I do believe that there are fixed moments that act as anchors. If we look back on our lives, only one small change, and we could have had an entirely different life. Not just yours, but the decisions that your parents made, led to you being born. What if they made a choice that led to them meeting other people? Had the housing market not crashed, I may have been a real estate agent. (I was looking into it.) Instead, it did crash, and I had been dumped and ended up making a last minute decision that ultimately led to this very book. What I am trying to say in a very round about style, do not feel as if anything is inevitable for better or worse.

"**I need to have people like me**." This is not true. It is nice when people like you, but the fact is that if they do not see the value in themselves, they will have a difficult time seeing your value. I learned very quickly that I have a polarizing personality. People either really like me or really don't. There are very few in the lukewarm category. I am rather blunt and some do not resonate with that. It is something that I had to make peace with a long time ago, which was very liberating. When you decide to start speaking your truth, you may lose friends and family at first, but suddenly you will begin to attract the ones who also resonate with your truth. You are your own person, with your own opinions and needs. When you find your "tribe" and find yourself surrounded by supportive, like minded individuals, then you have indeed found a treasure. As each of you grow and expand, you will find that either you grow closer or further. Growing further is not a bad thing, because it means that each of you is already attracting someone else who vibrates with the new ideas and patterns. In the end, the only person who needs to like you is you. You can't force or manipulate others into liking you, because eventually they will see your true self and either love you or not. That is on them.

"You can't have it all." This is such a common saying that I would be surprised if you could find anyone that has not heard it before. There are people who have it all. They have families, career, health, happiness, but it takes planning and balance. It takes the ability to limit each, to prioritize, and to find the time for you. Perhaps you can't have it all, in the amounts of time that you would like, but until they invent the 36 hour day, we need to work with what we have. Workers, especially here in the U.S., need to start taking their maternity leaves and vacation time. Take the days when you need it or want it. If you are in a job that pressures you to give up that time or threatens your job security, then you may want to see if there are any positions or places that value its employees. There are laws in place to help, and if you do not use them, then the one to blame for the lack of balance is you.

I am speaking to the employers out there:

If you want a productive work staff, then pay them well; give them leave to be with their families, and to take care of themselves. Sick employees are not productive ones. Overworked employees burn out and leave.

There are plenty of companies and businesses that see the people who work for them as peers, not a number. My favorite bosses were the ones who jumped in and worked with us. They got in the mix and explained, not demeaned. They put health and family first. You were seen as family, this makes a huge difference. Surprisingly, those companies and their CEO's still did well on a financial level. Money was never an issue and neither was company loyalty. There was a place I worked where new owners took over; money became more important than the clients and employees. Turnover became very high, and the employees eventually stopped caring. I bring this up because they lost balance and thus started losing staff, clients and money. Law of Attraction is tricky. They focused on the lack of money, based on what they thought should be coming in. In the end, they lost the people who helped them to reach such a high level of success.

Having it all is about balance and once you commit to balance, everything else falls into place!

Chapter 10
What to Do with the Negative

As I said earlier, there will be a companion workbook to help you design your own plan for release. It is such an individual process, that for anyone to tell you this is exactly how to do it, is foolish. If you have a toolbox to turn to and a variety of things to try, then you will hopefully move through the process easier.

The first thing anyone needs to do is acknowledge that there are blocks in the first place. Again the L.O.A. community will negate this, saying that it creates more of what you do not want. I am turning it around and saying how can you create positive energy while you have not acknowledged the blocks buried deep or even the ones on the surface? To clear out the emotional, spiritual, and mental clutter is just as important as clearing out the physical. When you do not process and take note of all the things that are making it difficult to manifest what you want, then you are just adding to the frustration and inner clutter.

This is the step that primes you for release. The way you acknowledge it is through communication. You must communicate to yourself, all of the fears, ideas, anger, programs, situations and people that are adding to this block.

Example problem: I want a happy healthy relationship.

Step 1. Acknowledge

State the problem "I always date the same kind of person."
Q: Why has that been a problem?
A: They keep me at distance and do not make me a priority?
Q: How are you mirroring that behavior?
A: By not spending time with myself.
Q: Why do you do this to yourself?
A: I don't have enough time.
Q: Is it that you do not have enough time, or that you do not make yourself a priority?
A: A little of both.
Q: How does that make you feel?
A: Frustrated
Q: What's the solution?
A: Make more time for myself?
Q: How will you do that?
A: By eliminating something from my schedule.
Q: Can you do that?
A: I have to, if I want to develop a relationship with myself.

This is an example of how to communicate with yourself on a practical and emotional level. It may feel silly at first to ask yourself and then answer your own questions, but clear communication will help you to discover feelings and patterns that may have otherwise stayed hidden.

Another way is to work with a good coach or therapist. I ask some of the very same questions, when I am sitting with a client. I had to take those very same steps for myself. You can also talk with a trusted friend or family member. Do not underestimate a good old fashioned chat fest!

To begin with, it is also a good idea, not to let things build up. Do not make the same mistake I did, by waiting until it took a health crisis and panic attacks, to figure out that something needs to change. Physical activity, creative outlets, and feeling your feelings as they happen can help you release, before it has a chance to get stuck and become a more permanent fixture.

Step 2. Release

Now that you have taken notice of the issue at hand and hopefully had a good long talk with yourself, you can do the work of release. As I said before, this process can be a long or a short one. When something is stuck in your energy/thought patterns it can at first feel like work, but as it releases, it begins to feel freeing. The deeper the block is rooted, the longer or more times this step can take. It is a process, so be patient with yourself.

Another thing to take note of is: Are you still very emotional about the situation? If you are, you will want to wait until the sting has dissipated. You cannot fully release until your emotions have calmed and you have felt all the feelings there are to feel about this. If you are still raging, then you will feel completely ridiculous doing a release activity.

Giving yourself permission to let something go may be very helpful as we sometimes define ourselves by our blocks. I can't sing, I can't run, I can't leave, I can't stay... those are a lot of cant's and by saying them, you are defining and limiting yourself. Babies don't use that word until we give it to them. They learn with ease, and then we tell them things like stop, can't, don't, won't. You spend a year and a half excited for their first words, first steps and all of their other firsts. Then, almost immediately, you tell them to stop the very thing you were excited to see. Of course, limits for their safety are great and needed, but how is telling them to stop singing or making noise for their safety? It isn't, it's for your convenience. In a school setting it is different; there are a variety of children with many different needs. In this situation, you are setting boundaries for the group rather than an individual.

If you have children, by practicing allowing, you can also help yourself.
Your child wants too much Halloween candy three options other than the word "Can't"

1. Tell them that if they eat too much they could get sick.
2. Unfortunately if they, *do* try it and they get sick once, they will think twice about it the next time. (I lived that one. Never did that again!) They will learn to set their own boundaries and will understand why you warned them against it.
3. Remind them that if they eat it all now, then if they want some later, there will not be any for them.

Another option to use instead of "No," is "Not now. Let me give you three other times that will work better." This takes it from being a no, to giving them some choice and control. By doing this with yourself, you empower yourself to allow in what you want, without causing other issues. This happened to me the other day. The one area I am always trying to allow change is my weight, but I do enjoy yummy food. I had the most incredible breakfast the other day, but it was carb heaven. Rather than saying I need to never have this again or allowing myself to have one every day for the rest of my life, I told myself that I can have it again in a few months. It was allowing both a healthy decision and a delicious one at the same time. I will manifest that breakfast again, just not again and again and again.

Example problem: I want a happy healthy relationship.

An example of release for the problem above: State out loud or write it down on a piece of paper "I release the feelings of unworthiness and forgive all people and situations that gave me that thought, including myself. I forgive and release all exes and people who reinforced this program within me. I release all cords, thoughts and programs that kept me tied in that pattern. All is released with gratitude for the lessons learned and the love for making me stronger. I now take this energy back for myself and fill the newly opened spaces with healing light and unconditional self-love."

Notice how no names were named, it is not important to be specific, in fact it can be better to leave names out altogether. Identifying specific situations or offenders can reignite resentment and bad feelings.

Example number two is to get active; and the deeper the block the more physical you want to get.

Channel all of that energy into a healthy productive outlet. For deep hurt or pain: running, martial arts, kickboxing, and drumming are fantastic ways to move it out. Do check with a doctor to make sure that you are healthy enough for these activities. You can also attend a drumming circle, and you will get the benefit of surround sound healing! In the workbook, I will give more details to help you max out the benefits of each activity.

Once you have made the decision to let something go and allow the new in, you can't keep going back. It is a commitment that you make to yourself. This too takes practice. I can now speak of all of my exes without any emotion or anger. I released them completely, to the point that talking or even writing about it here, no longer brings up those old feelings. I can speak of those who have wronged me without even feeling the need to forgive, because I have and that is done now. So if I must speak of them I am not in that vibration any more. I have moved on.

To the outside world this could make you appear cold or uncaring, but that is not the case, it is that you are making your health and happiness a priority and are no longer allowing someone else or an old situation to cause you pain.

Step 3 Allow

This is the step where you are ready for what all of the seminars get you pumped up for, letting in the good. Once you have acknowledged and released the blocks, then allowing in positive manifestations becomes so much easier.

Allowing is recognizing that you are worthy of positive forms of abundance. All that you manifest could be seen in a positive light, but instead of wishing and hoping for things to happen for you, you can create the energetic environment that welcomes them.

Start by appreciating the small blessings: a found penny, an unexpected call from a friend, or your kids making their bed without you having to ask. You then go from appreciating to appreciating with the expectation of more. Not the kind of expectation that leaves you disappointed, rather the expectation that good has already entered your life and more is sure to come in its own time. The journey and anticipation is as much of the abundance, as is the actual event itself.

How many of you look forward to a holiday and the buildup only to find yourself a little blue the day that it's over? It happened to me. I went to a friend's wedding and was super hyped for it. I am at the age where weddings are fewer and farther between. I rarely have an occasion to get dressed up, and I spent weeks picking out the outfit and just looking forward to seeing them enter a new phase of their life. The day was beautiful. Everything was fantastic from top to bottom. I made sure to be in the moment and enjoy the company, the food, and the dancing. After it was over, instead of pining for the preparations that were so much fun, almost as much fun as the wedding, I threw myself into preparing for the next big event. I turned to the future and expected more fun and excitement to unfold on my path.

You see, the big event is only one moment, while the preparations leading up to it are many, and they are usually filled with joy and excitement over the culmination. This can happen when you graduate, go on a first date, or snag the job you always wanted. The moment you finally get what you want: What then? Never ending bliss? No, regular life kicks in, and you set your sights on something new. I once heard someone say, that the moment you are done remodeling or redecorating your house, it is time to start over. Isn't L.O.A like that? Once you have achieved what you wanted, you will inevitably want something else. Perhaps it is in another area, or an upgrade on what you have. This is not being greedy or unsatisfied; rather it is the act of allowing the flow of life, growth and expansion to occur.

When you are doing these three steps, there is another action that you can take to turn around the inner dialog. If you hear or feel yourself saying something negative, turn it around.

Examples: N= Negative P=Positive

N -"I am always late."
P - "Today I took my time, and from now on, I will give myself the joy of being early."

N -"My family makes me late."
P - "While my family gets ready, I will get other things done around the house."
P - "Maybe we avoided something bad by being a little late."

N - "I never have enough money to pay all of my bills."
P - "I am so happy to have some money to pay what I can."
P - "This contrast shows me that I am ready to attract more financial abundance!

N - "My significant other never listens to me or pays attention to me."
P - "How can I pay more attention to myself?"
P - "While my significant other is busy, I am going to discover something fun to do!"

P - "I love that my significant other is independent and secure enough in our relationship to do things on his/her own."

N - "I never get enough sleep."
P - "I enjoy getting so much done while I am awake."
P - "I am committing myself to more sleep and better health!"

N - "There are so many crazy drivers, that it is scary."
P - "I am blessed that I am a safe driver and that am noticing who to avoid."

N - "This class is so difficult."
P - "I am learning so many new things in this class and can enjoy the challenge!"

These were just a few examples of how to turn around the inner or external dialog. Sometimes you can override frustrations and turn them into a beneficial experience. You have the power to choose how you react to situations and how you allow them to make you feel. It takes practice and consistency, but it pays off not only by what you begin attracting into your life, but how you begin to appreciate what is already in front of you.

Chapter 11

When to Work with a Professional and Which Kind

Dear Potential Client,

No one can tell you when you are ready to work with someone, except for you. First, you must look at the blocks.

Who can help?

Yourself: Some blocks you can take care of yourself!

- You know what the block is and where it came from.
- You have been able to work out your feelings on the situation.
- You can see all sides without becoming overly emotional.
- You are already successful at releasing past issues and moving forward.
- You are highly self-aware and objective about the situation.

There is a big difference between the following professionals and each serve a different purpose

Life Coach- A coach can help you in your development and working towards certain goals in multiple different areas of your life. They may be general or have specific specialties. They are not medical professionals.

- You have specific goals or areas you wish to develop.
- You have blocks, but may not have discovered them yet and need help identifying what they are.
- You are highly motivated and ready for change.
- You are good at working on your own and just need some tips, tools, and someone to work with occasionally.
- A good coach listens and allows you to take the lead.
- Your coach should not tell you what to do, but may help you to narrow down your options.
- They hold up a mirror to your life and ask you to look deeper.
- They help you to uncover your inner motivation.
- They help to uncover old programs and give you tools to release them yourself.
- Does not/ Should not offer advice
- Good for short/mid-term

Licensed Counselor

- Has a Master's Degree or Ph.D.
- Can range from specific specialties to general help
- Seen short to mid-term

- May or may not use psychotherapy as part of their services
- Helps to diagnose and uncover specific problems
- Deals with behaviors
- Acts as an advisor and works with the patient in a process of discovery
- Will offer advice specific to the problem.

Psychologist

- Ph.D.
- Extensive training in psychology and Psychotherapy
- Can administer a wide variety of tests
- Offers counseling and therapy
- Seen mid to long-term
- Offers advice and tools
- Works with mental illness
- Focuses on treatment with Behavioral Therapy.

Psychiatrist

- Medical professional
- Can prescribe medicine
- Often works in tandem with Psychologist
- May focus more on the physical responses of the mental illnesses and medicines
- Duties overlap with that of the Psychologist
- Seen long term

Also on the list are but not limited to:

- Nutritionist
- Physical Therapist
- Personal Trainer
- Marriage/relationship counselors

Mental illness and Medical conditions need Medical doctors. This does not mean that you can't also work with the other professionals listed above. However, a Counselor or Coach is not prepared nor qualified to take the place of a medical professional.

If you begin to work with a coach or counselor and they recommend that you work with a Psychiatrist or Psychologist or any other medical professional, it is not a rejection, rather an act of care. They are being smart and staying in their lane.

A personal trainer is not the same as a physical therapist. They have two very different jobs and training. If you are dealing with an eating disorder, a nutritionist can offer support, but they are not the first ones to seek for help. You should be working with a medical professional as well as a psychologist who specializes in your condition.

What does this have to do with L.O.A.? A lot actually. Removing your blocks can take a team and removing your blocks is a vital part of attracting what you want. In addition, happiness and inner peace brings you to a place of understanding; sometimes what you think you want is not truly what you wanted at all.

Money = Freedom, choice, movement

When you realize that you already have the power to move, make choices and free yourself, the actual money becomes less important.

Love = Self-love, acceptance, acknowledgement, attention

When you give these things to yourself, or take note of where it is already being given to you, then the love of a specific person becomes less important.

Success = Power, acknowledgement, achievement

You have power over your own life; power that is given to you can also be taken away. Focus on the power that you were born with. You are surrounded by loved ones who acknowledge you, now acknowledge yourself. You achieve things every day. When you focus on that you can redefine success and find that you already have it!

Part of the trick of L.O.A. is that you already have everything you need. Everything you want is laid before you ready to be noticed. When we look past the material world, we can see that everything is there for us. Money can be found, but will not bring you happiness, that comes from within. Love is everywhere, but love that is given can be taken away. The love you give yourself will and should always be put first. Inner peace is letting go of trying to control your circumstances and instead enjoy the ebb and flow of change in your life.

For my personal story:

- I wanted more space, because I was not making enough space for myself.
- I wanted more time, because I was not giving it to myself.
- I wanted more health, because I did not love myself enough to make healthy decisions.
- I wanted more money, but realized that I could choose to do anything and was already doing it!
- I wanted to find a soulmate, but realized that I have been surrounded by them my whole

life and started to give myself the love I craved.

Chapter 12

Final Thoughts

You are unique and this makes your journey just that, yours. I am a firm believer that there are no mistakes; even when the path you are on becomes full of questions, back steps, and obstacles, you are exactly where and who you are supposed to be. No apologies needed. Do not spend your life wishing and assuming that you are to be anything other than your perfectly flawed you. Know that your flaws are perfect because they make you who you are, and your dark side, your pain, and your problems can be the gift that helps you to rise and become stronger than you ever thought possible. Every misstep and challenge ultimately brings you to a better version of yourself, if you allow it. We are here to learn and grow, challenge can make that happen!

Law of Attraction is not some mysterious force that is bringing you closer or further from what you want. Instead, see it as a mirror of what you are feeling, thinking, and saying. Wanting = lack: The universe will give you more lack. Gratitude = abundance: The Universe will give you more to feed that feeling. When in doubt, find something already in your life that makes you feel blessed. I use the word Universe loosely, because in truth you are your own universe. Everything you perceive is from your point of reference; it is why pinning down a truth is difficult, because it always depends upon the point of reference.

You have the power to adjust your perspective and thus, your truth. So when the L.O.A. friends say just don't think about it; if you have gone through the steps of acknowledge, process, and release, then that is a step you can finally take. Shift your perspective, find the positive side of the truth that lay before you (like the Negative Blessings chapter talks about) and with that new perspective, you can peacefully move your mind to a different part of your life that is already flowing in the direction that makes you happy.

It is healthy to question and think for yourself. I encourage you to ask; "How does this apply to my situation? Does this information feel right to me? Does this book, person, advice etc. bring me closer or further from my truth? People will try to pass on their wisdom, and that is a beautiful thing. However, do not allow that wisdom to make you feel less than, or feel as if you *SHOULD,* be doing something differently. Your gut, and what you are attracting, will tell you if it is time to make a shift or change.

Changing, letting go, and release are never a failure, instead they are a sign that you are taking the time to listen you your needs. Taking that step should be commended and celebrated, as often we hold on trying to make something work that is no longer meant to be in our energy. I can't tell you

how many people I have known, who justify and
make excuses for staying in situations that bring on
stress and anxiety. They stay as if they can fix it or
make it work, when in reality they are keeping
better situations at bay. They don't want to be seen
as someone who gave up. They see it as a weakness
and worry about how others will view them. Once
they did let go, and allowed themselves to be free,
they were amazed to see how many blessings flew
in to their lives. They made space. I say this to
remind you, that in moments of frustration, to stop
and see what you can let go of to make room for
some of those new blessings.

The Companion Workbook will offer activities and
exercises to help you listen to your gut and look
within. There will be activities for each part of the
process: Acknowledge, Release and Allow. It is
easy to be lost or overwhelmed by all the
information that is out there. The important
information is what you can take from yourself.
Learning about yourself, is a journey worth taking.
It is my sincerest hope that what you have read here
or in the workbook can make that journey simpler
and easier. To get you started on the path of action I
have included a code for a free mini workbook on
page 4.

What you have read here may or may not be the
answers that you were seeking. No book, no

teacher, no guru has all the right answers for you, but they can help you build a plan that does work for you. Use the tools at your disposal and more importantly, use your beautiful mind. Do not say I can't, instead say I haven't yet. Do not close your eyes to the possibilities that lay before you. And if you feel that those possibilities rise like an impossible mountain, then take it one step at a time and enjoy the journey, remembering the journey is also a gift.

Made in the USA
Monee, IL
12 August 2023